26
Lively LETTERS

26 Lively LETTERS

Making an ABC Quiet Book

Barbara Williams and Carol Grundmann

Taplinger Publishing Company • New York

Published in the United States in 1977 by
TAPLINGER PUBLISHING CO., INC.
New York, New York

Published simultaneously in the Dominion of Canada by
Burns & MacEachern Limited, Ontario

Library of Congress Cataloging in Publication Data

Williams, Barbara.
    26 lively letters.

    1. Textile crafts. 2. Alphabets. 3. Books.
I. Grundmann, Carol, joint author. II. Title.
TT699.W54   746   76-13328

ISBN 0-8008-7918-X

Introduction

A quiet book is a symbol of love. First there's the love of the child for a book carried about affectionately until the pages are soiled, the colors faded, and the last button loose from its threads. But there's also the love the adult has put into the book in hours of creative effort, anticipating those moments when a quiet book will be needed.

Fortunately, small children are no longer expected to be seen and not heard *all* the time. But occasions still exist when noisy exuberance is inappropriate. Therefore the wise parent who must take a small child on a long trip by plane or car or even a short trip to a church, restaurant, or doctor's waiting room will plan ahead by providing an interesting toy which the youngster can play with quietly. Such a toy should be small, light, varied, colorful, noiseless, and reasonably indestructible. These requirements are perfectly met by so-called "quiet" books, or handmade fabric books filled with a wide range of tricks or movable parts which the child can manipulate all alone.

The following pages offer patterns for a quiet ABC with 26 varied activities designed to hold the attention of even the most adventurous and squirmy youngster. The completed book will make an excellent gift for a child, a new mother, or a kindergarten teacher. It will also be a very popular bazaar item if you care to make several.

Preparing the Pages

With the following instructions you can make a 28-page book of 26 alphabet letters, plus a title page and a blank back page. The completed book is fairly bulky, and the 26 alphabet pages also require considerable time to make. You may therefore decide to eliminate some of the designs and make a smaller, less time-consuming book. If you do this, pick an even number of the designs you like best and do not do the alphabet letters at the top of the page. Nor do you have to pay any attention to the order in which the book is put together as you do in the alphabet book.

You may also want to cut down the time required for making a book by eliminating some of the procedures described in the accompanying instructions. Most people who are making quiet books want to create lovely gifts that are both durable and beautiful and are consequently willing to spend several hours in the construction of each page. You can, however, greatly reduce the time by (1)

eliminating all lettering, (2) making all appliqué from felt rather than woven fabric, (3) gluing rather than sewing felt appliqués in place, and (4) omitting Pellon reinforcement from detachable pieces such as acorns (stitches for snaps will therefore show).

Materials and Tools Needed

Pages: 1⅞ yards of 44-inch fabric (purchase extra fabric for testing)
Cover: 10-inch by 20-inch piece of vinyl plastic or heavy fabric
Ruler
Pencil
Cardboard
Scissors
Pinking shears

Transfer pencil (available at most craft stores and sewing counters)
Felt-tip markers, colored crayons
White glue
Paper punch
Sewing machine (preferably zigzag)
Other items listed with individual patterns

Selecting the Materials

Any solid-color cotton fabric is suitable for the pages of a quiet book, although pastels are easier to work with than bright colors. You may want to use several different pastel shades, alternating them throughout the book. However, an off-white fabric such as unbleached muslin is more versatile than a colored one and will save you trouble in the long run.

Of more importance than the color of the fabric is the way it responds to ink and crayon, particularly if you want to transfer the lettering to the fabric pages of your book. If you will test your material with several different kinds of felt-tip markers before you begin, you will save yourself great anxiety later on. Most felt-tip pens will not work. Their ink smears as it is applied to the fabric and washes out completely when water or juice is accidentally spilled on it. For testing, choose only those pens labeled "not water soluble." Write several words on the fabric, the same size you intend to make your final lettering. Let the ink set for a few minutes and then hold the fabric under running water.

If you have difficulty finding a pen that suits you, you may decide to rely mainly on colored wax crayons. Although they are somewhat coarse for lettering, they

work very well on most fabrics for coloring large designs. Some stores sell crayons made especially for fabrics, but regular crayons work nearly as well. Use a heavy pressure and avoid any white spaces between strokes. Lay the decorated fabric between two clean pieces of heavy brown paper and press with a hot iron. The heat will force the color into the fabric, and the brown paper will absorb excess wax. Do not reuse the brown paper, or the colors will smear.

After you have tested the fabric, pens, markers, and crayons for their suitability, purchase the colors and quantities you will need. As indicated above, each ABC quiet book requires 1⅞ yards of 44-inch fabric. Now you are ready to continue the steps outlined below.

Making the Pages

1. Measure and cut from light cardboard a rectangle measuring 8 inches by 16 inches. This is the pattern for two finished pages of the quiet book, each measuring 8 inches by 8 inches. Make a small notch at the exact middle of the top and bottom. This will indicate the inside margin of your 8-inch by 8-inch pages. Sketch the vertical line between the two notches lightly in pencil. Then when you make each individual page, you can place your design so it is not too close to the inside margin of the book.

2. Lay the cardboard rectangle on the fabric and trace around it carefully with a pencil. Do this 14 times. Leave at least 2 inches between the rectangles as you draw them on the fabric.

3. Cut out the rectangles approximately 1 inch outside the lines you have traced. *Do not cut on the lines.* You need not cut evenly at this point in the preparation of the quiet book because you will cut again later with pinking shears. You now have 14 rectangles, which will make 28 finished pages.

4. If you are making an alphabet book, you must do the designs side by side as listed below. If you do not use the alphabet letters from the designs, you can arrange them in any manner you choose.

LEFT HALF OF RECTANGLE	RIGHT HALF OF RECTANGLE
blank (last page)	title page
A airplane	Z zoo
Y yarn.	B banana
C circus	X Xmas

W	wings	..........D	dinosaur
E	earrings	V	valentine
U	ukulele	..........F	flowers
G	game	..........T	tree
S	spiders	..........H	hands
I	igloo	..........R	rabbit
Q	queen	..........J	jack-in-the-box
K	kite	..........P	pelican
O	owl	L	lace
M	mirror	..........N	nose

Transferring the patterns

Many of the patterns in this book are regular patterns and can easily be traced from the book, cut, and pinned to the fabric you are working with. But some are drawings such as the clown in C for Circus or the pirate's features in E for Earrings and have to be reversed. And if you don't want to do your own lettering freehand, all the lettering must be reversed. You can do this in several ways.

1. Trace each drawing or lettering you want to use from this book to a sheet of white paper. You can use thin, see-through paper which you place on top of the pattern.

2. Place the hand-traced pattern upside down on a sheet of plain white paper. (The plain paper will help you see the drawing or lettering better.) Go over the design or lettering very carefully on the back with a transfer pencil, making a backward design.

3. Place the pattern on the fabric. Pin it in position so it will not slip while you are transferring it by iron.

4. Set your iron to "cotton." Use a press cloth or a sheet of clean heavy paper between the iron and the tracing to prevent scorching. Be sure that the side marked with the transfer pencil is next to the fabric.

Or for the lettering, you can trace it on a thin piece of white paper. Put the tracing pencil side to the glass of a window with good light. Then put another piece of paper over it and trace the lettering with a transfer pencil and continue as in the first method.

And occasionally when there are just a few details, as in the felt-tip marking on the zebra in Z for Zoo, you can punch holes in the paper pattern with a sharp, soft, lead pencil which will give you guide marks.

General Hints for Success

TITLE PAGE. Compose your own title page using, wherever feasible, the names of the recipient and the giver. For example, the picture shown of Tammi's ABC Book.

DETACHABLE PIECES. Small detachable pieces, such as acorns and Christmas-tree ornaments, will last longer and look better if you take the trouble to follow all the steps in the instructions accompanying the individual pages in the book. You may, however, prefer to save time by eliminating the Pellon reinforcement and sewing the snaps or Velcro directly to the felt.

PRINT FABRIC APPLIQUÉS. A few appliqués of bright cotton prints, although time-consuming to make, will add variety to your quiet book. Unless you have a zigzag sewing machine, however, they are hardly worth the effort. Even with a zigzag machine, they require considerably more time than felt appliqués. For these reasons, specific instructions for making print fabric appliqués with a zigzag sewing machine appear only with patterns C (circus), Y (yarn), and Z (zoo). You may, of course, wish to use them elsewhere in a quiet book you are making.

FELT APPLIQUÉS. Appliqué designs from colored felt are easier to apply than those made from cotton prints, but they are less versatile. They also have the disadvantage of adding considerable bulk to the finished quiet book. Felt appliqués can either be glued or sewn in place, but small children, who do not understand that some of the designs in a quiet book are intended to be removable and some are not, will try to peel off any felt which is merely glued in place. Machine stitching is therefore recommended in the specific instructions throughout this book.

ALPHABET LETTERS. If you are doing an alphabet book, you may find it safer to trace the alphabet letters onto 1-inch by 1½-inch rectangles of bright-colored vinyl, and when the lettering has been completed, glue the rectangle in place. This will keep you from making a mistake on the actual fabric page. If you are not satisfied with the lettering, discard the rectangle and do another one.

PAINTED DESIGNS. To avoid unnecessary bulk in your quiet book, you can substitute painted designs for felt appliqués, using either fabric tube paints or less expensive colored crayons. Tube paints require a steady hand and a mechanical device (such as a large embroidery hoop) for holding the material taut. Practice on a sample piece of your fabric before you apply any paint to a quiet book page. Crayons are far safer to use. See the section headed "Selecting the Materials" for instructions on applying wax crayons to fabric.

REINFORCEMENTS. Repeated use of snaps, Velcro, eyelets, etc. can cause damage to your quiet book pages if the fabric is not reinforced with material such as fusible Pellon or iron-on tape. Instructions accompanying each pattern suggest appropriate reinforcements to prolong the life of your quiet book, but you may omit them if you wish.

WHITE GLUE. Opaque white glue (by any of several brand names) has at least three advantages over pins in securing felt to any other fabric before machine stitching: the felt is less likely to slip or pucker, you are less likely to break a sewing machine needle, and you don't have to waste time removing pins when you are through. Use the glue in very small dabs, however, or it will show on the finished product.

A sample title page. You can compose your own for a particular child

A for Airplane. This airplane is bright green felt with a red propeller, but any other contrasting color combination can be used. It is best, though, to use black felt behind the cutout windows. The propeller is attached with a paper fastener and can be twirled around and around.

MATERIALS

Black felt for the airplane windows
Felt (color is optional) for the airplane
Felt or vinyl (color is optional) for the propeller
Heavy cardboard ½ of an inch by 3¼ inches
1 brass paper fastener
White fusible Pellon or iron-on tape

METHOD

1. Trace the paper pattern of the airplane and the window backing.

2. Pin airplane pattern right side up on top of the felt and cut around the outline and holes for windows.

3. Using the pattern provided, put a piece of black felt to fit behind holes for windows.

4. Hold black felt in place with a few dabs of white glue so it will form the windows.

5. Place the airplane on the page, following the photograph, and being careful to keep it away from right margin.

6. Trace pattern for propeller to heavy cardboard and cut out. Cover entire surface of cardboard propeller with a thin layer of white glue. Glue cardboard propeller to felt or vinyl and place under a heavy weight. (Do not cut out the felt or vinyl until glue is thoroughly dry.) While glue is drying, continue with other steps.

7. Machine-stitch airplane to fabric page, sewing around outside edge of airplane and around the edges of windows.

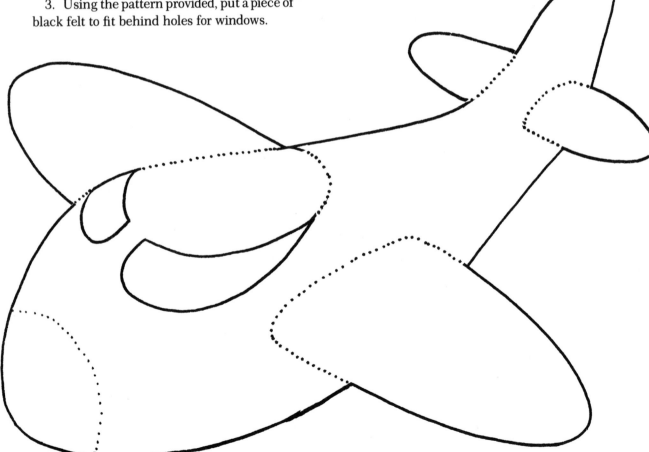

14

8. On wrong side of fabric page, reinforce the nose of the airplane with a circle of fusible Pellon or iron-on tape about 1½ inches in diameter.

9. Remove cardboard propeller from beneath weight, and cut the felt or vinyl so that edges are even with the cardboard. You now have a propeller of felt or vinyl reinforced with heavy cardboard.

10. Using a paper punch, make 1 hole in the middle of the propeller and 1 hole in the nose of the airplane. Then attach the propeller to the airplane with a brass paper fastener.

11. Follow the dotted lines of the airplane with a black felt-tip marker or with black thread and a narrow zigzag stitch on your sewing machine.

12. Add the lettering to the fabric page with a felt-tip marker. If you wish to trace the lettering, trace it on thin, see-through paper. Place the tracing upside down on a sheet of plain white paper. Go over the lettering with a transfer pencil, making a backward design. Turn over and transfer to the fabric.

Piece for under windows

Aa airplane

wind me up

B for Banana.   The top half of this yellow felt banana is secured by Velcro strips and can be peeled back to the stem.

Yellow felt
Yellow thread
Tan felt
Tan thread
Heavy-duty tan Velcro strip approximately
¾ of an inch by 7¾ inches
Heavy-duty Pellon
Fusible Pellon

METHOD

1. Trace patterns for top banana peel, bottom banana peel, and 2 stem ends of banana to a sheet of plain paper.

2. Pin the patterns for the top and bottom halves of the banana to yellow felt and cut along the lines.

3. Pin the 2 patterns for the stem ends of the banana to tan felt and cut along the lines.

4. Cut a piece of fusible Pellon somewhat larger than the whole banana and fuse it by iron to the wrong side of the fabric page where the banana will go.

5. With a few light dabs of white glue, secure the 2 stems of the banana and the bottom half of the banana (but not the top half) to the fabric page. Machine-stitch the 2 stem ends of the banana and the bottom half of the banana to the fabric page with matching thread.

6. Make a reinforcement for the top half of the banana peel by pinning the pattern to heavy Pellon and cutting around the edges.

7. Cut a strip of heavy-duty tan Velcro approximately ¾ of an inch by 7¾ inches. You will sew the fuzzy half of this double-thickness strip directly to the fabric page to resemble the fruit of the banana and the stiff half of the Velcro strip to the underside of the banana peel

to make the peel adhere to the fruit. However, the single strip of Velcro is too bulky to follow the curve of the banana, and the top and bottom ends need trimming. You must therefore shape the Velcro as described in steps 9 and 10. And as shown in the photograph.

8. Divide the double-thickness Velcro strip into 3 by cutting directly across in 2 places—once approximately 3¼ inches from 1 end and again approximately 2½ inches from the other end. These 3 pieces can now be set at slight angles to each other, following the curve of the banana. The longest strip will fit on the bottom, the next longest on the top, and the shortest in the middle.

9. Separate the 3 double-thickness Velcro strips so you have 6 pieces. With scissors, taper the top ends (1 end of 1 fuzzy piece and 1 end of 1 stiff piece) and the bottom ends (1 end of 1 fuzzy piece and 1 end of 1 stiff piece) so they will fit in place without showing under the banana peel.

10. Using a few dabs of white glue, secure the 3 fuzzy pieces of Velcro in place on the fabric page, curving them as necessary to fit within the lines.

11. Using a few dabs of white glue, secure the 3 stiff pieces of Velcro correspondingly on the heavy Pellon, curving them as necessary.

Make sure that the Velcro pieces on the page and on the reinforcement are set in opposite curves that will adhere to each other before you proceed.

12. Machine-stitch the fuzzy Velcro to the fabric page and the stiff Velcro to the heavy Pellon.

13. Using a few dabs of white glue, secure the yellow felt banana peel to the top of the heavy Pellon to which you have sewn the stiff Velcro. Make certain that the yellow felt matches the outline of the banana on the fabric page and that the 2 sides of the Velcro will mesh before you proceed.

14. Machine-stitch the heavy Pellon to the outside edges of the yellow felt banana peel with yellow thread.

15. Machine-stitch the very bottom of the felt banana peel to the fabric page, running the machine back and forth several times for extra strength.

16. Add the lettering to the fabric page with a felt-tip marker. If you wish to trace the lettering, trace it on thin, see-through paper. Place the tracing upside down on a sheet of plain white paper. Go over the lettering with a transfer pencil, making a backward design. Turn over and transfer to the fabric.

18

C for Circus. The tent and the circus clown look well in gay, bright colors. This circus tent is a small, yellow, turquoise, and white print, and the clown can be done in bright-colored felt and crayons of reds, oranges, hot pinks, and bright blue and yellow.

MATERIALS

Orange, yellow, brown, or black felt (for clown's hair)

Bright-colored felt in 3 or 4 shades (for flag, clown's collar, hair, and clown's pompons)

Thread to match felt above

Cotton print fabric approximately 12 inches square

Nylon coil zipper to match print fabric above (see step 8)

Thread to match print fabric above

Colored crayons

METHOD

1. Trace the drawing of the clown to a sheet of thin, see-through paper. Place the hand-traced pattern upside down on a sheet of plain white paper to help you see it better. Go over the design very carefully on the back with a transfer pencil, making a backward design.

2. Following the placement in the photograph, transfer pattern to fabric page by iron.

3. Trace on paper the patterns for tent and flag. Also trace the patterns for clown's hair, clown's collar, and clown's pompons which you wish to do in felt.

4. Color with wax crayons all the portions of the clown for which you do not intend to make felt appliqués. Press with a hot iron between two sheets of brown paper.

5. Using the patterns you have traced, cut clown's hair, collar, and pompons from felt.

6. Glue or machine-stitch felt appliqués to fabric page.

7. Fold print fabric in half and cut along fold. Machine-baste a wide (at least ⅝ of an inch) seam along edges you have just cut to prepare for installing the zipper. Press.

8. You will need a zipper about 5½ inches long. Since packaged zippers do not come in this length, you will have to cut one to size. Measure 5½ inches from the edge of the closed

20 nylon zipper (not the edge of the tape) and run your machine back and forth several times. You can now cut your nylon coil zipper just outside the machine stitching.

9. Install zipper in print fabric so that it opens from the bottom up. Leave room at the bottom for a hem and follow instructions that come with the zipper for a centered (not lapped) application. Hem bottom by machine.

10. Trace tent pattern to a clean sheet of paper. Center tent pattern on fabric on top of zipper so that highest point lies on center seam above zipper and bottom edge is even with hem of fabric. Pin.

11. Cut around edges of tent along lines for sides and top and pin tent to fabric page over clown.

12. Stitch tent to fabric page along sides and top (not bottom) with a narrow and loose zigzag stitch. Set zigzag stitch to a wide and tight setting. Go around the sides and top again, covering the first stitching. Second stitch should extend beyond print fabric, covering raw edges.

13. Cut a flag from colored felt, using the pattern, and lightly glue felt flag in place at top of tent. Machine-stitch felt flag in place.

14. Add the lettering to the fabric page with a felt-tip marker. If you trace the lettering, follow the instructions in steps 1 and 2.

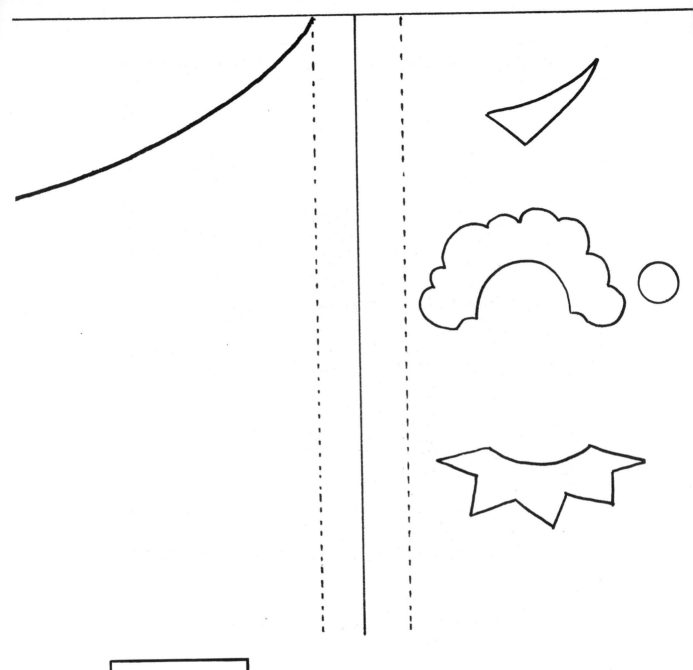

Cc circus

look inside

D for Dinosaur. The spikes of this felt dinosaur can be formed by lacing the shoelace through the eyelets. The only small difficulty with this page is that when you assemble the book, you must leave spaces open on the border. Full instructions for this are given in the chapter on assembling.

MATERIALS

Felt for dinosaur's body (color optional)
Cotton fabric for testing (extra material like fabric pages)
16 eyelets (plus 2 or 3 extra ones for testing) and eyelet tool
27-inch shoelace
1 small button for eye

METHOD

1. Cut the pattern for the dinosaur in felt.

2. Place the felt dinosaur on the center of the page, keeping it far enough from the left-hand margin. With a pencil, mark the places for 8 eyelets about an inch above the dinosaur's back for the eyelets which will make the spikes. Follow the photograph for the placing of the eyelets.

3. Test the extra eyelets with the eyelet tool on the extra material to see how many layers of reinforcement (if any) your fabric page requires.

4. If your fabric pages are thin and require

24 reinforcement, cut out small pieces of material and pin them on the wrong side of the fabric page, underneath the marks for the eyelets.

5. Place the felt dinosaur on the page and make 8 eyelets, following the placing in the pattern.

6. Take 1 end of a 27-inch shoelace to the wrong side of the fabric page, at either the left or the right of the 16 eyelets. A right-handed child will go from right to left. The end of the shoelace should therefore be tacked in place underneath the button eye. (You can sew the eye and the shoelace at the same time.) A left-handed child will go from left to right. The end of the shoelace should therefore be tacked in place underneath the tail of the dinosaur at the far left of the page. (You can sew the eye in place in a separate maneuver.)

7. Pull the shoelace through the nearest eyelet to which it is attached, either the one near the eye or the one near the tail. And then sew around the outside edge of the felt body.

8. Add the lettering to the fabric page with a felt-tip marker. If you wish to trace the lettering, trace it on thin, see-through paper. Place the tracing upside down on a sheet of plain white paper. Go over the lettering with a transfer pencil, making a backward design. Turn over and transfer to the fabric.

NOTE: Both a right-handed child and a left-handed child will need to have access to the underneath side of this page from both the left and the right. Instructions for assembly, therefore, explain how to leave hand space on the bottom and the right.

dinosaur Dd

lace my spikes

E for Earring. This pirate's ear is reinforced and the earlobe is semiattached so the earring can be fastened and unfastened. He looks properly fierce with a black hat and eyepatch and a red bandanna under his hat, but the colors can be changed.

MATERIALS

Flesh-colored felt
Flesh-colored thread
Black felt or vinyl
Black thread
Red felt
Red thread
Heavy Pellon
Metal ring fastener

METHOD

1. Trace patterns for hat, head bandanna, eyepatch, face, and ear reinforcement on a sheet of paper. Note that the whole face, including the ear, will be cut from one piece of felt but that only the ear needs reinforcement.

2. Pin the face pattern on flesh-colored felt and cut around edges.

3. Trace the pirate's features in dotted lines on the felt.

4. Pin and cut 2 layers of reinforcement for the pirate's ear—1 from heavy Pellon and 1 from flesh-colored felt. Glue the 2 layers of reinforcement under the pirate's ear so that the Pellon is hidden by felt on the top and felt on the bottom. Set under a heavy weight to dry while you proceed.

5. Pin bandanna pattern to red felt and cut around edges.

6. Pin hat pattern and eyepatch pattern to black felt or vinyl and cut around edges.

7. Remove face with reinforced ear from beneath weight. Machine-stitch around edge of ear. Punch a hole in earlobe.

8. With a few dabs of glue, secure the pirate's face in position on the fabric page, following the photograph. Do not put glue under pirate's ear.

9. Machine-stitch pirate's head to fabric page around outside edges with one exception. Do not go around the outside edge of ear. Instead, sew along the pirate's cheek inside his ear, leaving the ear to hang free.

10. With a few dabs of glue, secure pirate's head bandanna in position on the fabric page, following the placement in the photograph. Machine-stitch bandanna to page. As you sew around the edge, you will attach the top of the pirate's ear to the fabric page, but the earlobe, where earring will be fastened, will still hang free.

11. With a few dabs of glue, secure pirate's hat in position on the fabric page, following the placement in the photograph. Machine-stitch hat to page around outside edge.

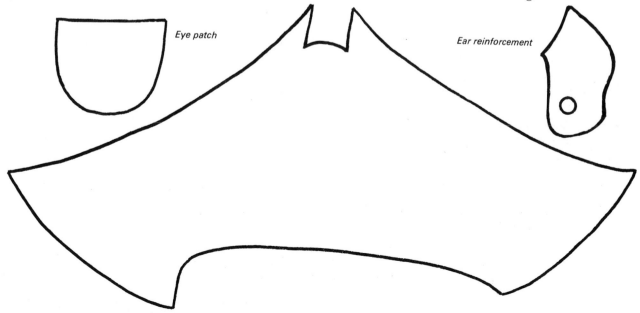

Eye patch

Ear reinforcement

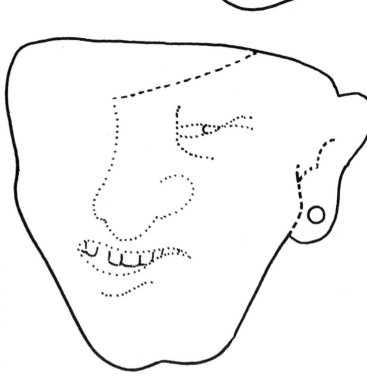

12. With pins—not glue—secure pirate's eyepatch in position on the fabric page. Machine-stitch along bottom curve of eyepatch but not the straight edge at the top. This will make one of several pockets in the finished quiet book where you can occasionally hide special treats for the child like raisins, nuts, or sugarless gum.

13. With a pencil, draw a line from top of eyepatch over pirate's brow to represent string on eyepatch. Go over the line with a narrow zigzag stitch on your sewing machine. If you use a machine, set the stitch to narrowest width and very tight setting. Pin a plain sheet of paper underneath fabric page, so the fabric will not pucker as you sew. Pull off excess paper when you are through.

14. Put the paper pattern on the felt face and punch through the paper at the dotted lines with a sharp pencil. This will give you guidelines for the features. Go over the pirate's features with felt-tip markers. Add whiskers with felt-tip pen if you wish.

15. Put metal ring fastener through hole in pirate's ear.

16. Add the lettering to the fabric page with a felt-tip marker. If you wish to trace the lettering, trace it on thin, see-through paper. Place the tracing upside down on a sheet of plain white paper. Go over the lettering with a transfer pencil, making a backward design. Turn over and transfer to the fabric.

flowers Ff

make me grow

F for Flowers. The child can make these flowers "grow" by pulling them up. The horizontal crossbar at the end of each stem keeps the flower from coming out completely so it cannot be lost. The felt at the bottom which covers the stems can be either brown or tan for earth or green for grass. These particular flowers were done in orange with a yellow center for the daisy, red for the tulip, and lavender for the hyacinth with small purple blossoms. But any flower-like colors are equally effective.

MATERIALS

Tan or brown felt for soil or green for grass
Tan or brown or green thread to match felt
Green felt for stems and leaves
Orange, yellow, red, lavender, and dark purple felt (colors optional)
Heavy cardboard

METHOD

1. Trace the patterns for the parts of the flowers on a sheet of paper. Trace these on heavy cardboard and cut out with scissors.

2. Cover the stems and leaves with white glue. Turn the cardboard stems and leaves upside down on a single piece of green felt. Set them under a heavy weight while glue dries and proceed with next step.

3. Cover the cardboard flower heads with white glue. Turn them upside down on colored felt. Use orange felt for the daisy, red felt for the tulip, and lavender felt for the hyacinth or any other colors you wish, set the flowers under a heavy weight.

4. While they are drying, cut a piece of tan or green felt 7¾ inches by 3¼ inches. At this stage and before you sew the felt down on the fabric page, you might wish to add the lettering for "make me grow" (see step 13). Then if you make a mistake, you can always cut another piece of felt.

5. Remove stems from beneath weight. With fine-tip scissors, cut the green felt around the stem and leaves of each flower so that the felt exactly matches the cardboard reinforcement.

6. Remove flowers from beneath weight and cut around cardboard with fine-tip scissors and add center for daisy with yellow felt and buds for hyacinth in dark purple. Glue in place.

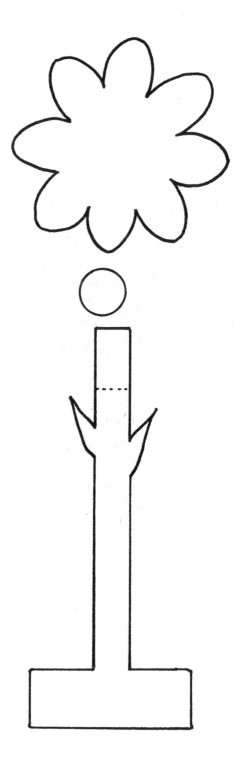

Glue flower heads to stems a generous ½ inch down the stem.

7. Set flowers on page where you think they look best. Do not glue.

8. With a ruler, measure 8 inches from the right margin to find the center of the double fabric (marking the midway spot).

9. Using a few dabs of glue, secure the felt in position at the bottom of the page over the flowers. The left edge of the felt should extend almost to the midway spot you have just measured. Be careful not to put any glue near the flowers, or you will prevent their moving freely as they "grow."

10. Set pins in the felt to indicate where machine stitching along the top edge should go. Machine-stitch along the top edge of the felt in accordance with pins. On each side of each flower, run the sewing machine back and forth for extra strength in the stitching where it is likely to work loose in time.

11. Machine-stitch along the left edge of the felt, across the bottom and up the right.

12. Trace and color the caterpillar with felt-tip markers or crayons.

13. Add the lettering to the fabric page with a felt-tip marker. If you wish to trace the lettering, trace it on thin, see-through paper. Place the tracing upside down on a sheet of plain white paper. Go over the lettering with a transfer pencil, making a backward design. Turn over and transfer to the fabric.

G for Game.   In this game the felt markers have Velcro fasteners which will adhere quite well to the felt game board. The looped part of the Velcro fasteners are sewn to the fabric page beneath the numbered disc as is shown in the photograph. These secure the markers when the child is not playing with them. The colors here are optional. This particular page was done with a mustard-yellow game board and bright, contrasting markers.

5 different colors of felt
5 colors of thread to match felt
4 Velcro fasteners
Colored posterboard
Popsicle stick
Brass paper fastener
Heavy Pellon

1. Trace the patterns of the game markers. Use a ruler for the pattern of the game board to keep the lines of the outline straight.

2. From colored posterboard, trace and cut 2 circles for the base of the spinner. Spread the 2 cardboard circles with glue, and paste 1 on top of the fabric page and 1 directly under-

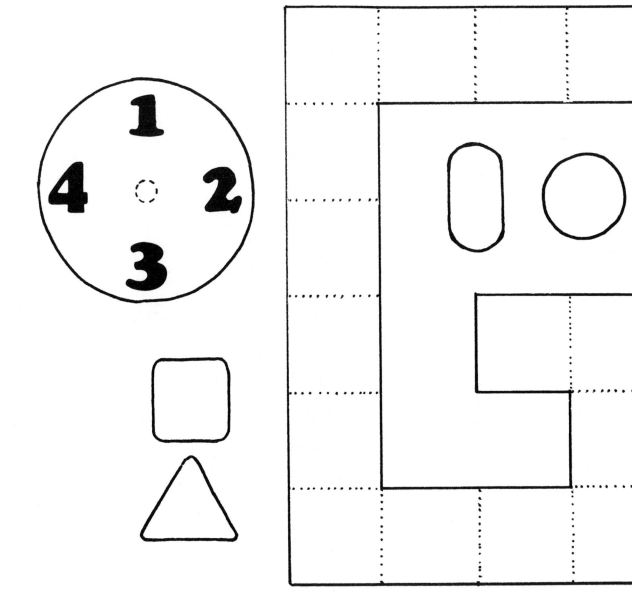

neath it on the bottom of the fabric page for added support. Follow the photograph to place these. It is a good idea to put the game board down, too, to see that you have plenty of room. Set the cardboard circles under a heavy weight for 8 hours or longer. If you remove the weight too soon, the double application of glue will cause the cardboard to buckle. Continue with other steps for this page and proceed with other pages while the glue is drying.

3. With a small hacksaw cut off a piece about 1¼ inches long from a Popsicle stick. The round end of the Popsicle stick makes a good pointer, so you will want to drill your hole near the square end. Drill a ⅜-of-an-inch hole.

4. Pin the game board pattern to a piece of felt and cut around the outside edges. With a ruler and felt-tip marker, draw a starting zone, an ending zone, and fifteen 1-inch squares as shown on the pattern in dotted lines.

5. Trace the 4 shapes for the game markers on a piece of heavy Pellon. Sew the stiff halves of 4 Velcro fasteners inside the shapes you have traced on heavy Pellon. Cut out the 4 Pellon shapes.

6. With light dabs of glue, secure the 4 Pellon shapes to 4 different colors of felt. Cut out the 4 different pieces of felt to match the 4 Pellon shapes they are glued to. Machine-stitch the Pellon and felt of each game marker

together, sewing carefully around the outside of the shape.

7. Remove fabric page from beneath weight (after 8 hours or more have elapsed). Machine-stitch the fuzzy halves of the 4 Velcro fasteners beneath the cardboard circle.

8. With a few dabs of glue, set the felt game board in position on the fabric page. Machine-stitch the game board to the fabric page around the outside edge of the felt.

9. With a felt-tip marker, draw 4 numbers on the cardboard circle as shown in the picture.

10. Measure the center of the cardboard circle and punch a hole through both layers of cardboard and the fabric between them with a sharp object. Loosely attach the Popsicle stick spinner to the cardboard circle with a brass paper fastener. Test to make sure the stick will spin when it is flipped with a forefinger. Put the felt game markers in position, attaching them to their matching Velcro pieces.

11. Add the lettering to the fabric page with a felt-tip marker. If you wish to trace the lettering, trace it on thin, see-through paper. Place the tracing upside down on a sheet of plain white paper. Go over the lettering with a transfer pencil, making a backward design. Turn over and transfer to the fabric.

H for Hands. This can be an easy page to make depending on how you do the numbers for the clock face. You can also dispense with the colored felt hands on the ends of the clock hands.

Colored felt (1 or 2 colors) for clock cabinet and hands
Felt for clock numbers (optional)
Thread to match felt
Stiff cardboard
Brass paper fastener
Fusible Pellon

METHOD

Before proceeding, decide by what method you want to affix the numbers to the clock. The easiest method is by felt-tip marker. The numbers in the photograph were colored with crayon. This method is not the best for areas as small as the numbers on the clock because crayons will smear slightly when heat is applied to fix them. The most attractive method, but the most difficult, is to cut the numbers from felt and then glue or sew them to the face of the clock. If you use felt numbers, you will not have to trace the numbers on the face of the clock. Instead, you need only make 12 marks around the face of the clock to indicate where you will set the felt numbers later.

1. Trace the patterns for the clock hands and stems and the clock cabinet on a sheet of paper. Pin the clock cabinet pattern to a piece of colored felt and cut around the outside line. Cut around the inside circle, making a hole in the middle of the felt.

2. With a few dabs of glue, secure the clock cabinet in position on the fabric page, checking with the photograph for the placement. Machine-stitch the clock cabinet to the fabric page along the outside edge and the inside circle.

3. Make the colored numbers for the clock by whatever method you choose, felt-tip marker, crayons, or felt. Crayons must be pressed with a hot iron between 2 layers of brown paper.

4. Trace the clock hands on heavy cardboard and cut with scissors. Cover the cardboard hands with glue and place upside down on a piece of colored felt. Place under a heavy weight until dry.

5. When dry cut around the hands and punch a hole near the end of each stem. If you wish you can add felt hands of a contrasting color by following the pattern for the separate hands.

6. With ruler and pencil, find the center of the clock face. Cut a small circle of iron-on tape and attach it to the back of the fabric page. Cut a small hole in the center. Attach the 2 clock hands to the clock with a brass paper fastener inserted through the holes punched in the stems and the clock face.

7. Add the lettering to the fabric page with a felt-tip marker. If you wish to trace the lettering, trace it on thin, see-through paper. Place the tracing upside down on a sheet of plain white paper. Go over the lettering with a transfer pencil, making a backward design. Turn over and transfer to the fabric.

what's the time

I i igloo

build me

I for Igloo. The igloo can be made in two ways. If the child is old enough, safety pins can be used to fasten the igloo blocks. For younger tots, you can use snaps. Because the safety-pin method is more complicated, the instructions are given here. If you wish to use snaps, their placing is indicated on the pattern. And if you use snaps, you do not have to back the whole fabric page with Pellon. Small circles of Pellon under each snap on the fabric page will give enough strength. Nor, if you use snaps, will you have to follow the note in the section, ''Assembling the Book'', about leaving an opening on the finished page when you assemble the book.

MATERIALS

White felt
White thread
Heavy Pellon
Snaps or 8 safety pins, approximately 1″ long.
Fusible Pellon

METHOD

1. Trace all lines of the igloo blocks on a piece of heavy Pellon.

2. Using a zigzag stitch on your sewing machine, attach a safety pin to each square block of the Pellon igloo. Wherever sizes will permit, sew the safety pin horizontally in the middle of the block. For right-handed children, the head and point of the pin should point right. For left-handed children, the head and point of the pin should point left. (Note that you are working on wrong side of the finished block, so these directions will eventually be reversed.)

3. Put a dab of glue on each Pellon block, on the opposite side of the fabric to where you have sewn each pin. Place the Pellon blocks (not yet cut out) on a piece of white felt until glue dries.

4. Using zipper foot of sewing machine, sew Pellon and felt of each block together just inside the pencil lines on the Pellon.

5. Cut along the lines of the Pellon blocks, creating blocks of 2 thicknesses—felt and Pellon.

6. Transfer the igloo pattern to the fabric page, if desired, with a felt-tip marker so the

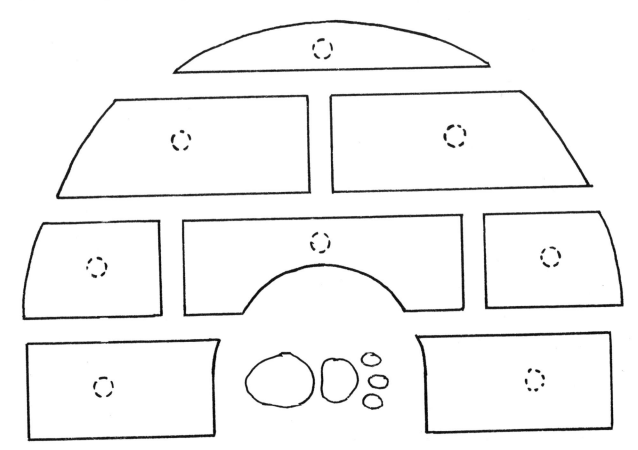

child can see the order. Use a ruler in order to keep your lines straight.

7. Fuse a 9-inch by 9-inch piece of Pellon on the back of the igloo page. (Do not attempt to fuse the Pellon while safety pins are attached to the page.)

8. Trace the pattern for the footprints. Transfer them by making a backward pattern with a transfer pencil. Or place the pattern directly on the fabric page and make guidelines by piercing the outline with a sharp lead pencil. Then fill with felt-tip marker.

9. Add the lettering to the fabric page with a felt-tip marker. If you wish to trace the lettering, trace it on thin, see-through paper. Place the tracing upside down on a sheet of plain white paper. Go over the lettering with a transfer pencil, making a backward design. Turn over and transfer to the fabric.

build me

open my lid

J for Jack-in-the-box. Either vinyl or felt can be used to make the front of the box and the lid. Vinyl was used here, as it is a little stronger and will stand up better under use. The colors for the box and the felt collar should be strong and bright. Here the box is red vinyl and a bright pink was used for the collar.

MATERIALS

1 color of felt or vinyl for the box
3 or 4 other colors of felt
Thread to match
2 tiny buttons for eyes
1 larger button for fastener
Length of elastic cord to go around button fastener (approximately 1½ inches)

METHOD

1. Trace the 2 patterns for the box on a sheet of paper. Place the patterns on the fabric page according to the photograph. Make guidelines for the side of the box.

2. Trace, cut, and pin the collar pattern to a piece of felt and cut along the lines. With a few dabs of glue, secure the clown's collar to the fabric page in the center of the open box. Machine-stitch the collar to the fabric page around the outside edges.

3. Trace, cut, and pin the face pattern to a piece of felt and cut along the lines. With a few dabs of glue, secure the clown's face in the center of his collar. Machine-stitch the clown's face to the fabric page around the outside.

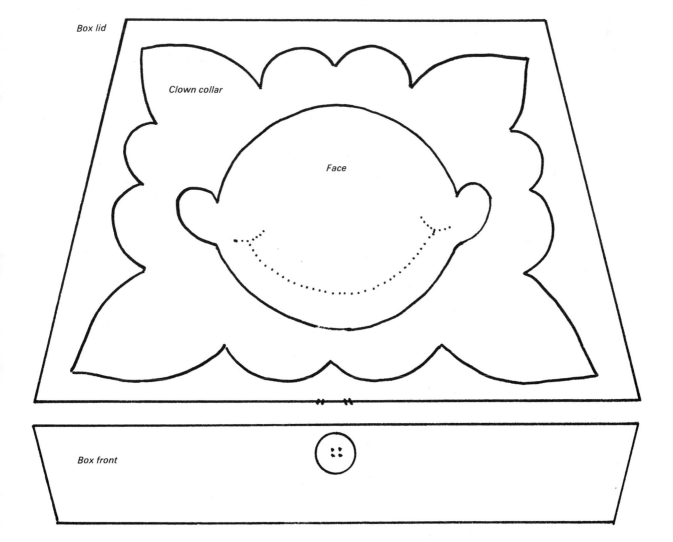

4. Pin the clown's nose to a piece of felt and cut around the circle. With a dab of glue, secure the clown's nose in the center of his face. Machine-stitch or tack the clown's nose to the fabric page.

5. Pin the patterns for the eye designs to a piece of felt and cut around the edges. With 2 dabs of glue, secure the eye designs to the clown's face. Sew the 2 tiny buttons through the eye designs to the fabric page.

6. Draw the clown's mouth indicated with a dotted line with a pencil. Go over the clown's mouth with a felt-tip marker, or machine-stitch the mouth with a narrow zigzag stitch.

7. Pin the 2 parts of the box to colored felt or vinyl and cut along the lines.

8. With a few dabs of glue, secure the front panel of the clown's box to the fabric page. Machine-stitch the front panel of the clown's box to the fabric page.

44

9. Sew a button on the front panel of the clown's box, halfway in from each side and about ⅔ of the distance up from the bottom.

10. Loosely set the lid of the box in position to determine how long the elastic cord must be in order to wrap around the button fastener. Pin the cord in place.

11. Cut a small piece of vinyl or felt the same color as the lid to reinforce the machine stitching for the elastic cord.

12. Spread the felt or vinyl reinforcement with a thin layer of glue and attach it to the underside of the lid with elastic cord in the middle.

13. Machine-stitch the elastic cord in place, sewing through the lid and the reinforcing felt or vinyl.

14. Set the box lid in position. Pin. Machine-stitch along the top (not the sides) of the lid.

15. Open the lid. Using a ruler, draw the right and left sides of the box with a felt-tip marker or narrow zigzag stitch to match color of the box.

16. Add the lettering to the fabric page with a felt-tip marker. If you wish to trace the lettering, trace it on thin, see-through paper. Place the tracing upside down on a sheet of plain white paper. Go over the lettering with a transfer pencil, making a backward design. Turn over and transfer to the fabric.

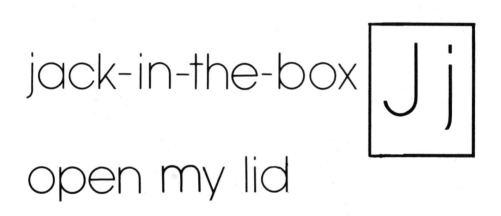

jack-in-the-box J j

open my lid

K for Kite. Though a simple page, it will give small children much pleasure. The body of the kite can be made from any scrap of bright felt. The ties on the kite's tail can be grosgrain ribbon if you have some or small pieces of printed materials.

Colored felt

Thread to match felt

Contrasting thread for kite string and support sticks

3 lengths of grosgrain ribbon ¾ inch wide and 6 inches long or 3 strips of print fabric cut to these specifications with pinking shears.

METHOD

1. Trace the kite pattern on a sheet of paper. Pin it to a piece of colored felt and cut around the outside edges.

2. With a few dabs of glue, secure the felt kite in place on the fabric page, following the photograph for the position. Machine-stitch around the outside edge of kite.

3. Take a pencil and draw 2 crossed, curved lines on the felt kite to represent support sticks, following the dotted lines on the pattern. Go over pencil marks for support sticks with felt-tip marker or with a narrow, tight zigzag stitch in a contrasting color. Draw with pencil a line following the kite's tail in the photograph. Place contrasting thread on sewing machine, using the same narrow and tight zigzag stitch. Prepare to sew the tail of the kite. Take a sheet of plain paper and put it beneath your fabric page as you sew so fabric won't pucker.

4. Take 1 fabric strip or grosgrain ribbon and find the middle of the 6-inch length. Pinch the ribbon or fabric strips through the width so that the ribbon is narrower in the middle than it is elsewhere. Machine-stitch along line for kite string with ribbon underneath.

5. About ⅓ the distance down the kite string, stop your machine and attach another length of ribbon. Attach another ribbon farther along the string, as in the photograph.

6. Add the lettering to the fabric page with a felt-tip marker. If you wish to trace the lettering, trace it on thin, see-through paper. Place the tracing upside down on a sheet of plain white paper. Go over the lettering with a transfer pencil, making a backward design. Turn over and transfer to the fabric.

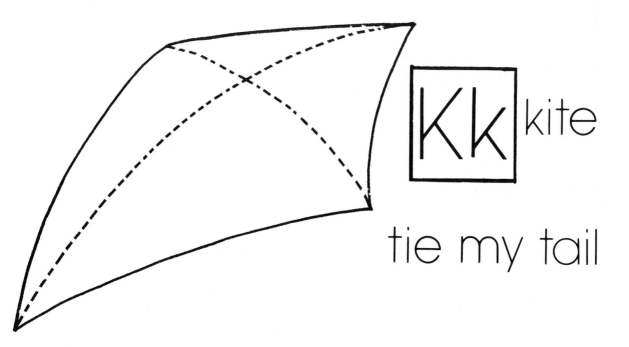

lace L l

lace me

L for Lace.   This shoe pattern requires some work, but it does make a handsome and durable page. For the shoe and the shoe's tongue, you should use vinyl or felt and dark colors—red, black, navy blue, or dark green—are best. That way a white zigzag stitch will show up nicely.

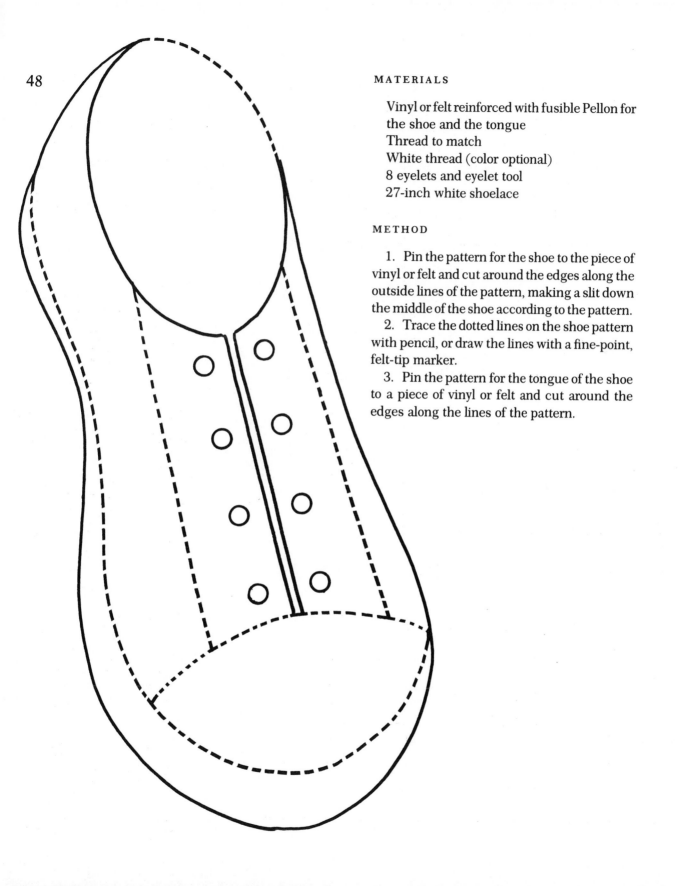

48

MATERIALS

Vinyl or felt reinforced with fusible Pellon for the shoe and the tongue
Thread to match
White thread (color optional)
8 eyelets and eyelet tool
27-inch white shoelace

METHOD

1. Pin the pattern for the shoe to the piece of vinyl or felt and cut around the edges along the outside lines of the pattern, making a slit down the middle of the shoe according to the pattern.

2. Trace the dotted lines on the shoe pattern with pencil, or draw the lines with a fine-point, felt-tip marker.

3. Pin the pattern for the tongue of the shoe to a piece of vinyl or felt and cut around the edges along the lines of the pattern.

4. Using white thread and a narrow, tight zigzag stitch (or straight stitch, if necessary), topstitch the dotted lines you have drawn on the shoe.

5. Place the shoe on the fabric page according to the photograph, being careful to keep it away from left-hand side of the page. Then put the tongue in place. Remove shoe and pin the tongue down. Machine-stitch along the bottom.

6. With an eyelet tool, insert 4 eyelets on each side (8 in all) of the slit down the middle of the shoe. Line eyelets up opposite each other as evenly as possible.

7. Pin the shoe in position on the fabric page and machine-stitch around the outside edges. Continue stitching around the back of the shoe along the line for the heel.

8. Insert shoelace in eyelets.

9. Add the lettering to the fabric page with a felt-tip marker. If you wish to trace the lettering, trace it on thin, see-through paper. Place the tracing upside down on a sheet of plain white paper. Go over the lettering with a transfer pencil, making a backward design. Turn over and transfer to the fabric.

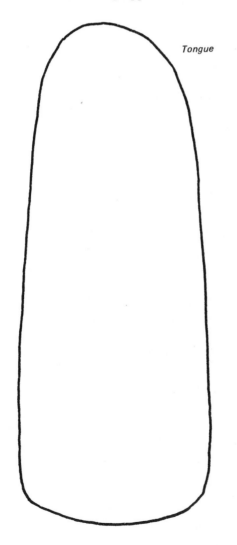

Tongue

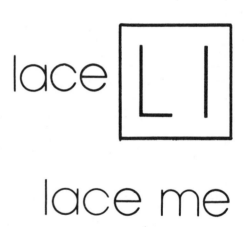

lace Ll

lace me

M for Mirror. The pink felt face unbuttons and falls down to reveal a round pocket mirror which is glued to the fabric page. For a very small child you may not wish to use a mirror, though one of good quality is quite safe. If you are hesitant you can substitute a round piece of Mylar.

MATERIALS

Brown or yellow felt for hair
Thread to match
Pink felt for face
Pink thread (optional)
Colored felt for collar
Black felt for bow tie
2 buttons (approximately ⅞ inch) for eyes
5-inch round mirror
Fusible Pellon

METHOD

1. Trace the patterns for the hair, face, collar, and bow tie to a sheet of paper and cut.

2. Place the face pattern on the fabric page following the photograph for the placement. Put mirror underneath so sides of face and mirror combine. Glue mirror on fabric page and set under a weight to dry while you proceed.

3. Pin the pattern for the hair to a piece of brown or yellow felt and cut around the edges along the lines of the pattern. Cut a slit on each side along the dotted line at the top to make the boy's bangs.

4. Reinforce the bangs with fusible Pellon.

5. Sew 2 buttons at the crosses on the bangs for the eyes.

6. Cut 1 collar pattern. Pin the patterns for the collar to felt and cut around the edges along the lines of the pattern.

7. Glue the felt collars to the fabric page, covering the bottom curve of the mirror.

8. Glue the hair to the fabric page, covering the top curve of the mirror. *Do not put glue on bangs, as this part of the felt should be left free.* Set under weights to dry.

9. Fuse a piece of Pellon to pink felt to make the boy's face. Pin the pattern for the face to the pink felt fused with Pellon and cut around the outside edges of the pattern.

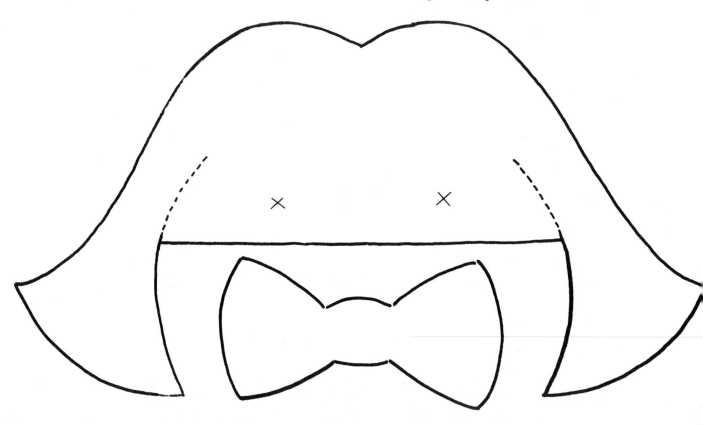

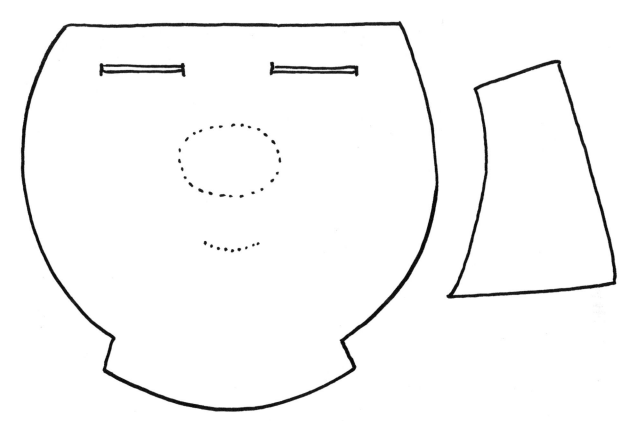

10. Set the boy's face lightly in place on the page to see where to make holes for the buttons. Measure and mark buttonholes with ruler and pencil. Make buttonholes in the pink felt with buttonhole attachment on your machine or with scissors only. Small children will have a little difficulty manipulating the buttons, so buttonholes should be extra long.

11. Put glue on the underside of the neck and glue in place on the fabric page, covering the bottom tip of the mirror. If you have correctly attached the hair and the face, they will overlap each other and button at the top to form the face and will swing open widely to expose the mirror.

12. Pin the pattern for the bow tie to black felt and cut around the edges along the lines of the pattern. Glue the bow tie in place on the fabric page, covering the boy's neck. You may have difficulty making the bow tie lie flat at the

top. If so, you can sew it by hand along the top with a needle and black thread. Do not worry about sewing the bottom.

13. With matching thread in your machine, sew around the entire outside edges of the hair, collar, and bow with a loose, wide zigzag stitch or plain straight stitch. This step is important in order to prevent the weight of the mirror from pulling all the felt pieces loose from the page.

14. Cut the pattern for the nose and place on the pink felt and trace around with felt-tip markers. Draw a curve for the mouth.

15. Add the lettering to the fabric page with a felt-tip marker. If you wish to trace the lettering, trace it on thin, see-through paper. Place the tracing upside down on a sheet of plain white paper. Go over the lettering with a transfer pencil, making a backward design. Turn over and transfer to the fabric.

N for Nose. There are two different ways of doing this page. You can use some felt for the main features as was done in the photographed page. Or you can trace the profile and the features and fill in the coloring with crayons. Whichever you do, small children will love endlessly shaping various noses from the chain.

54

MATERIALS

Various scraps of colored felt (optional)
Thread to match felt (optional)
Thread to match fabric page
1 piece of thin chain 6 to 7 inches long
(available at most craft supply stores, or you
can also use an old key ring or an old piece of
jewelry)
2-inch square of fabric for reinforcement

METHOD

1. Trace man's profile and hat to a sheet of
white paper. Place the hand-traced pattern
upside down on a sheet of plain white paper to
help you see it better. Go over the design very
carefully on the back with a transfer pencil,
making a backward design. Transfer the pattern to a fabric page by iron.

2. Color the man's hat and profile with
felt-tip markers and/or crayons. Apply crayon
strokes with heavy pressure. Leave the space
between the man's eye and the top of the upper
lip blank. If you used crayon for coloring, place
the fabric page between 2 pieces of brown
paper and press with a hot iron.

3. If you are using colored felt pieces, cut
from patterns for hat, eyebrow, eye, and lips.
Glue or machine-stitch to the profile.

4. Pin the 2-inch square of fabric to the wrong side of the fabric page for reinforcement under the stitching for chain.

5. Sew 1 end of chain to front and bottom tip of man's eye. Sew other end of chain to top of man's upper lip.

6. Add lettering with felt-tip markers. Use the same transfer method you used for the features.

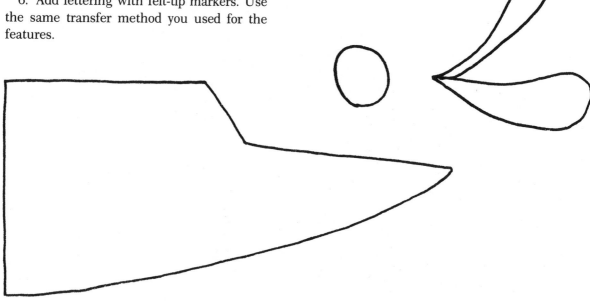

nose Nn

shape me

O for Owl. The owl can shut both eyes or wink with either. Button eyes are covered with buttonhole-type slits in the eyelids which are easily opened and shut. You can make him of any colors you wish. Here he has a brown body, black eyelids, red eyebrows, and a yellow beak.

MATERIALS

Felt in various colors large enough to make
the pattern pieces
Thread to match
2 eye buttons (available at most craft stores
and some fabric stores)
Fusible Pellon

1. Trace the separate patterns for the parts on a sheet of paper.

2. Pin the pattern for the owl's body to a piece of felt and cut around the edges along the lines of the pattern. With a few dabs of glue, secure it in position on the fabric page, following the photograph for the placement.

3. Machine-stitch the owl to the fabric page by sewing around the edges of the felt.

4. Cut a piece of fusible Pellon about 2 inches by 3½ inches and fuse it by iron to a piece of felt for the eyelids.

5. Using the round pattern, cut circles from reinforced felt for the owl's eyelids. Cut the 2 circles in half according to the pattern to make 4 semicircles. Machine-stitch along the straight edge of each semicircle.

6. Set the semicircles together in pairs to form eyelids on the owl's head. Place straight sides of semicircles vertically with a slight space between them to resemble circles with vertical slits. The slits will serve as buttonholes later. Pin in position.

7. Machine-stitch the 2 felt eyelids to the owl's head by sewing around the outside of each circle. Do not machine-stitch along the vertical slits.

8. Pin the pattern for the owl's eyebrow to a piece of felt and cut along the lines of the pattern. With a few dabs of glue, secure the brow to the owl's head above the eyes. Machine-stitch the brow to the fabric page.

9. Pin the pattern for the owl's beak to a piece of felt and cut along the outside lines. With a dab of glue, secure the owl's beak between and under the owl's eyes, so it touches them. Machine-stitch the owl's beak in place.

10. With a needle and thread, sew the eye buttons inside the 2 vertical slits of semicircles.

11. Add the lettering to the fabric page with a felt-tip marker. If you wish to trace the lettering, trace it on thin, see-through paper. Place the tracing upside down on a sheet of plain white paper. Go over the lettering with a transfer pencil, making a backward design. Turn over and transfer to the fabric.

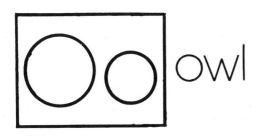

open my eyes

P for Pelican.   The pelican is like a jigsaw puzzle. All the pieces except the narrow upper beak, which is sewn on the fabric page, are attached with snaps. And there is a button and buttonhole for the eye. He can be taken apart and put together again time after time. You can use various colors of felt for the different parts. This pelican was done in light orange, dark orange, yellow, red, and black to complement the owl which he faces when the book is completed.

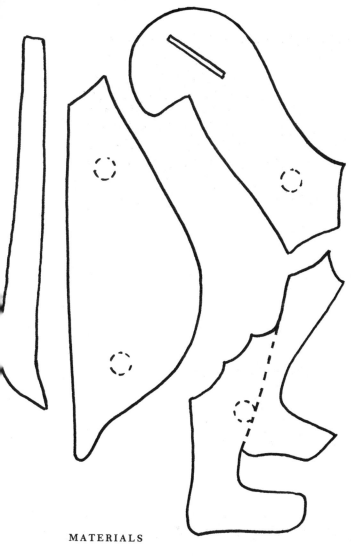

Any 5 colors as desired for the head, wing, body, feet, and the two parts of the beak
Thread to match
Heavy Pellon
White thread
1 plain button or 1 eye button (available at most craft stores and some fabric stores)
9 snaps

METHOD

1. Trace the separate patterns for the parts of the pelican to a sheet of paper.

2. Pin the pattern for the long, narrow piece of the pelican's beak to the felt you have chosen for the beak and cut around the edges.

3. All other parts of the pelican require Pellon reinforcement. Pin the patterns one by one to the Pellon and cut along the edges.

4. Put the concave halves of each snap aside for later use, sew the 9 convex halves of the snaps on the wrong (reverse) sides of the Pellon pieces, following the dotted circles in the pattern.

 body—3 snaps in triangle shape at far points
 wing—2 snaps at far ends
 wide beak—2 snaps at far ends
 feet—1 snap in middle
 head—1 snap at bottom of neck

5. With a few dabs of glue, secure each of the Pellon parts to a piece of felt. Place glue on the opposite side of Pellon to the one with the snap and lay them on the different colors of felt. The lower wide beak should match the upper narrow beak.

6. Machine-stitch around the edge of each Pellon piece. If you have sewn the snaps too close to the edges you may have to use a zipper foot. Machine-stitch across the feet, following the dotted line to indicate two feet. Cut the felt pieces with scissors so that the edges of the felt are even with the edges of the Pellon.

7. Place the pieces of felt on the fabric page following the photograph. With a few drops of glue secure the thin upper beak to the page. Mark the place the button eye will go on the fabric page and mark the buttonhole for the eye on the Pellon reinforcement of the head.

8. Remove the other pieces and machine-stitch the upper beak around the outside edge to the fabric page.

9. Sew the button directly to the fabric page in the correct position for the eye. Cut a slit for the buttonhole. Machine-stitch around the slit for the buttonhole with a regular straight stitch.

10. Fasten the head to the fabric page by means of the button and buttonhole. With a pencil, mark the spot on the page where the convex half of the snap should attach to the concave half of the snap.

11. Sew the concave half of the snap in position on the fabric page.

12. With a pencil, mark the correct spots for the concave snaps which will attach to convex snaps on the body, the lower wide beak, and the feet. Sew the concave snaps to the fabric page as marked.

13. With a pencil, indicate the correct spots on the back of the pelican for the concave snaps which will attach to the convex snaps on the wing. Sew the concave snaps to the body as marked on the pattern.

14. Add the lettering to the fabric page with a felt-tip marker. If you wish to trace the lettering, trace it on thin, see-through paper. Place the tracing upside down on a sheet of plain white paper. Go over the lettering with a transfer pencil, making a backward design. Turn over and transfer to the fabric.

pelican Pp

take me apart

Q for Queen. The crown for the queen is attached with a Velcro fastener so she can be crowned. The scepter made of a Popsicle stick slides up and down in her hand. If you are worried about two detachable pieces on this page, you can always make a round ball for the bottom end of the scepter matching the color of the top of the scepter and using the same method of two layers of felt and heavy Pellon glued together.

MATERIALS

Flesh-colored felt for the face and the hands
Gold-colored felt for the crown
Yellow felt for the diamond on the crown and the top of the scepter
Brown felt for the hair
Blue, white, pink, and red felt for the features
Purple or another color felt for the gown
Popsicle stick
Heavy Pellon
Velcro fastener

METHOD

1. Trace the separate patterns for parts of the queen to a sheet of paper.

2. Pin the pattern for the queen's crown to a piece of heavy Pellon and cut around the edges along the lines of the pattern.

3. Machine-stitch the stiff half of a Velcro fastener to the center of the queen's crown. Put the fuzzy half aside.

4. Spread a thin coat of glue on the Pellon crown (the opposite side to the one where you have sewn the Velcro fastener) and stick it to a piece of gold-colored felt. Place the crown under a heavy weight while glue dries and proceed with other steps.

5. For added strength, make the top of the queen's scepter from 3 layers of fabric: 2 layers of yellow felt and 1 layer of heavy Pellon. Pin

the pattern to the fabrics named and cut around the edges. Spread a thin coat of glue on each of the 2 felt layers you have cut for the top of the queen's scepter. Glue the Pellon layer and the tip of the Popsicle stick between the 2 felt layers and set under a heavy weight until glue dries.

6. Pin the pattern for the queen's face on a flesh-colored felt and cut around the edges on the lines of the pattern. Do the same with the colored felt for the queen's gown.

7. Arrange the face, the gown, and the scepter on the fabric page, following the photograph for the position. See that it is not too near the right side margin.

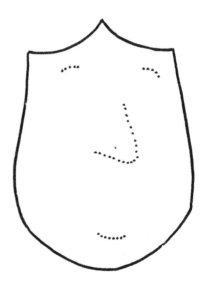

8. Remove everything from the fabric page except the face and secure it in position on the page. Machine-stitch the face to the fabric page around the edges.

9. Pin the pattern for the queen's hair on brown felt and cut around the edges along the lines of the pattern.

10. With a few dabs of glue, secure the queen's hair in position on the fabric page. Machine-stitch the queen's hair to the fabric page around the outside edges.

11. Using the small patterns for the features of the queen's face, cut eyes from white felt, pupils from blue felt, rouge marks from pink felt, and mouth from red felt. These facial features are too small for machine stitching, so glue them carefully in position on the queen's face, following the placement in the photograph.

12. Draw the queen's eyebrows, nose, and chin dimple with a felt-tip marker.

13. With a few dabs of glue, secure the queen's dress to the fabric page. Machine-stitch the queen's dress to the fabric page around the outside edges.

14. Pin the pattern for the queen's hand to flesh-colored felt and cut around the edges along the lines of the pattern. Cut a reinforcement for the queen's hand of heavy Pellon, using the same pattern.

15. With a few dabs of glue, attach the reinforcing piece to the felt hand for the queen

and set under a heavy weight while you proceed with other steps.

16. Remove the queen's crown from beneath the weight and cut around the edges, making the felt match the Pellon.

17. Using the small diamond-shaped pattern, cut a decoration for the queen's crown from a contrasting felt. Glue the diamond shape to the center of the queen's crown.

18. Remove the queen's hand from beneath the weight. With a light dab of glue near the knuckles, set the queen's hand in position on the fabric page.

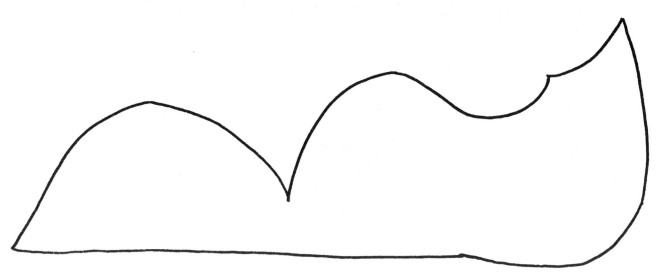

19. Remove the queen's scepter from beneath the weight. Slip the scepter under the queen's hand at an angle that looks as if she is holding it. (Compare the angle with the angle in the photograph.) Take a pencil and trace along both sides of the Popsicle stick on top of the queen's hand. Remove the scepter from beneath the queen's hand.

20. Machine-stitch the queen's hand in position in two maneuvers as follows: (1) Set needle into fabric at the top of the left parallel line and sew down the line and around the knuckles, stopping where you began; (2) Set the needle into fabric at the top of the right parallel line and sew down the line, around the top of the sleeve, and up the hand to the point where you began. If you complete these maneuvers correctly, you have made a slot under the queen's hand the right size and at the right angle to hold the scepter.

21. Place the crown on the queen's head according to the photograph. With a pencil, mark where the fuzzy half of the Velcro fastener should go on the fabric page. Machine-sew the fastener in place.

22. Add the lettering to the fabric page with a felt-tip marker. If you wish to trace the lettering, trace it on thin, see-through paper. Place the tracing upside down on a sheet of plain white paper. Go over the lettering with a transfer pencil, making a backward design. Turn over and transfer to the fabric.

queen

crown me

R for Rabbit. The rabbit pops in and out of a magician's top hat. The more care you put into the sewing of the rabbit, the more endearing he will be. Otherwise this is a very simple page. If 4½-inch long, 1-inch wide black grosgrain ribbon is hard to come by, you might substitute a length of black vinyl on a black felt top hat or a piece of black satin hemmed all the way around on a vinyl or felt top hat.

MATERIALS

White felt
Heavy white Pellon
1 thin white pipe cleaner 6 inches long
2 small pink buttons for eyes
White or off-white or pale gray thread
Pink thread
Black felt or vinyl
1 piece of 1-inch black grosgrain ribbon 4½ inches long
Black thread

METHOD

1. Trace the pattern for the hat on a sheet of paper.

2. Pin the pattern for the hat to a piece of black felt or vinyl and cut around the edges along the lines of the pattern. Also cut the hole at the top.

3. With a few dabs of glue, secure the black grosgrain ribbon to the black hat just below the brim, as shown in the photograph. Trim the edges of the ribbon to match the edges of the

hat. Machine-stitch the ribbon to the hat along the 2 long edges but not along the 2 short widths.

4. Pin (do not glue) the hat in position on the fabric page, using the photograph as a guide. Machine-stitch the hat to the fabric page all around the outside edge. Also machine-stitch the top curve of the hole at the top. Do not machine-stitch the bottom curve of the hole.

5. Trace all the lines of the drawing of the rabbit to a piece of Pellon by putting the Pellon on top of the pattern and going over it with a pencil.

6. Pin the Pellon rabbit to another piece of heavy Pellon with felt in between. (The completed 3-layer rabbit will be both stiff and soft—easy for a child to move up and down.)

7. Using off-white or a very pale gray thread, set your machine to a narrow and tight zigzag stitch. (A straight stitch is less attractive but will do.)

8. Sew the 3 layers of fabric together by going over all the lines on the rabbit except the lines inside the ears, the nose, and the tongue.

9. Put pink thread on machine to complete the stitching on rabbit on the ears, nose, and tongue.

10. Sew pink buttons in place for eyes.

11. Cut the pipe cleaner into 6 slightly uneven lengths about 1 inch long. Glue the pipe cleaner pieces on rabbit's face for whiskers.

12. Add the lettering to the fabric page with a felt-tip marker. If you wish to trace the lettering, trace it on thin, see-through paper. Place the tracing upside down on a sheet of plain white paper. Go over the lettering with a transfer pencil, making a backward design. Turn over and transfer to the fabric.

rabbit Rr

find me

S for Spiders. Some small children will be fascinated to learn that spiders have eight legs, unlike other insects which have six. But whether they are budding naturalists or not, this makes a fine counting game.

spider legs opposite each other so that each spider will need 4 pipe cleaners to make 8 legs. Spread glue along about 1 inch in the middle of each pipe cleaner and set in position on the fabric page.

4. With a few dabs of glue, secure the felt bodies of the 2 spiders in position on the fabric page on top of the pipe cleaners.

5. Machine-stitch around the edges of the felt spider bodies. You may have to use a sturdy needle in your machine and a long stitch in order to prevent your sewing machine needle from breaking as it goes over the pipe cleaners.

6. With a pencil, place 2 marks on 1 spider head and 1 mark on the other spider head to

MATERIALS

Felt (2 colors)
Thread to match felt
3 buttons for eyes
8 lightweight pipe cleaners, each approximately 6 inches long

METHOD

1. Trace the patterns for the spider bodies to a sheet of paper.

2. Pin 1 spider body to colored felt and cut around the outside edges. Pin the other spider body to the other piece of colored felt and cut around the outside edges.

3. Place the felt bodies of the 2 spiders on the fabric page according to the photograph. Mark the points the legs should extend outward lightly with a pencil. Remove spider bodies. Each pipe cleaner will serve for the 2

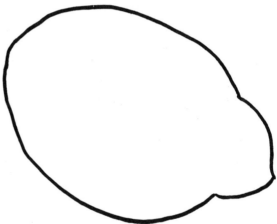

indicate the positions for the eyes, as shown in the photograph. Sew the eyes in place.

7. Bend the 16 exposed lengths of pipe cleaner to resemble the joints in the spider legs in the photograph.

8. Add the lettering to the fabric page with a felt-tip marker.

how many legs

T for Tree. The tree in this case is an oak tree, and the hollow trunk provides a place for hiding the acorns. The acorns don't have to be made with heavy Pellon, but they will stand up under wear and tear better if they are.

MATERIALS

Green felt
Thread to match
Brown felt
Thread to match
Light tan felt
Dark tan felt
7 snaps
Heavy Pellon

METHOD

1. Trace the patterns for the separate parts of the tree and acorns to a sheet of paper.

2. Pin the pattern for the top of the tree to green felt and cut around the edges along the lines of the pattern.

3. With a few dabs of glue, secure the top part of the tree in position on the fabric page, following the placement in the photograph, and machine-stitch the top of the tree around the outside edges.

4. Pin the pattern for the trunk of the tree to brown felt and cut around the edges along the lines of the pattern. Cut a hole in the trunk, as shown in the pattern.

5. With pins, not glue, secure the tree trunk in position on the fabric page and sew around the outside edges. You now have a pocket inside the tree trunk where the child can hide the acorns. This pocket also makes a good place to hide occasional treats for the child, such as raisins or nuts.

6. With a pencil, mark the 7 places on the

top of the tree for the snaps for the acorns. Put the convex halves of 7 snaps aside and sew the concave halves of the snaps to the 7 places you have just marked.

7. Take the acorn pattern and trace it 7 times with a pencil on a piece of heavy Pellon.

Sew the convex halves of the snaps in the center of the pencil marks on the Pellon outlining the acorns.

8. Cover the opposite sides of the acorns you have drawn on Pellon with glue, and set the piece of Pellon on a piece of light tan felt. Do not worry if you go over the edges of the pencil-drawn acorns. Too much glue is better than too little.

9. Set the 2 layers of fabric, felt side down, on a flat surface. Take 7 spools of thread the same height and put their holes over the prongs of the snaps. Place a heavy weight on top of the spools and proceed with next step.

10. From dark tan felt cut 7 cups for the acorns.

11. Remove Pellon and felt you have glued together from beneath heavy weight. Cut out the 7 acorns you have drawn.

12. Glue the cups to the bottoms of the 7 acorns and put the acorns back under a heavy weight as described in step 9 above.

13. Add the lettering to the fabric page with a felt-tip marker. If you wish to trace the lettering, trace it on thin, see-through paper. Place the tracing upside down on a sheet of plain white paper. Go over the lettering with a transfer pencil, making a backward design. Turn over and transfer to the fabric.

hide my acorns

U for Ukulele.   As this ukulele has to be reinforced with cardboard to keep the elastic cord strings taut, it makes a slightly bulky page. But to a very small child's enjoyment, the strings can be plucked.

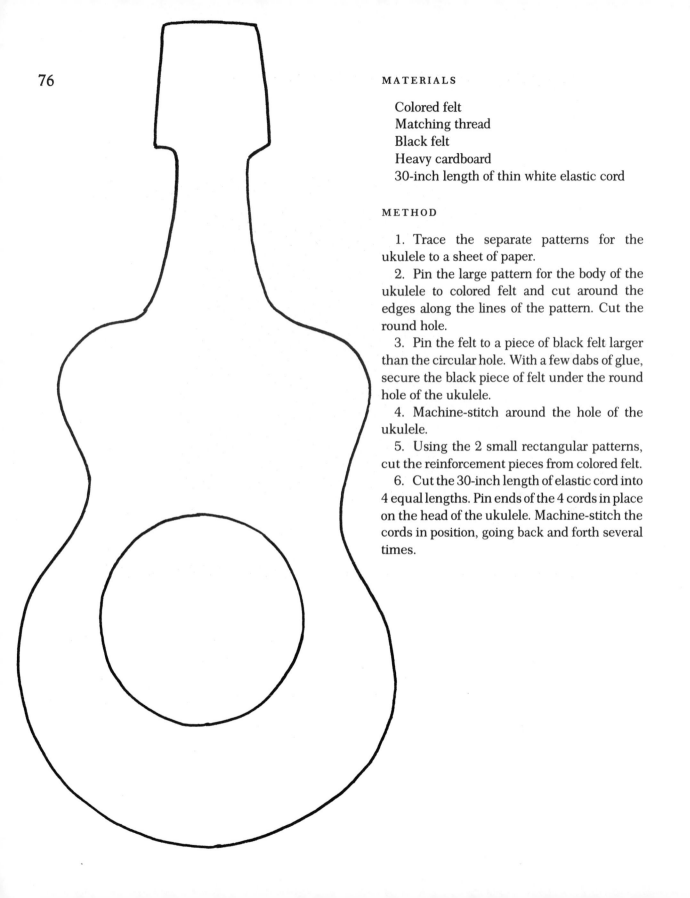

MATERIALS

Colored felt
Matching thread
Black felt
Heavy cardboard
30-inch length of thin white elastic cord

METHOD

1. Trace the separate patterns for the ukulele to a sheet of paper.

2. Pin the large pattern for the body of the ukulele to colored felt and cut around the edges along the lines of the pattern. Cut the round hole.

3. Pin the felt to a piece of black felt larger than the circular hole. With a few dabs of glue, secure the black piece of felt under the round hole of the ukulele.

4. Machine-stitch around the hole of the ukulele.

5. Using the 2 small rectangular patterns, cut the reinforcement pieces from colored felt.

6. Cut the 30-inch length of elastic cord into 4 equal lengths. Pin ends of the 4 cords in place on the head of the ukulele. Machine-stitch the cords in position, going back and forth several times.

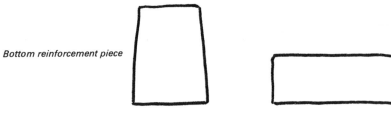

Bottom reinforcement piece

Top reinforcement piece

7. Pin the other ends of the 4 cords in place at the lower end of the ukulele. Fan the cords outward slightly as they go down the neck and pull them tightly so that they would make the fabric curl if you were not holding it.

8. Machine-stitch the cords in position, going back and forth several times.

9. With a few dabs of glue, secure the ukulele in position on the fabric page, following the placement in the photograph. Be careful to keep it away from the right margin. The tight cords will make the material curl, but do not worry about it.

10. Machine-stitch around the edges of the felt ukulele.

11. Trace the pattern for the ukulele to heavy cardboard with a pencil. Cut out the cardboard ukulele inside the lines so that it is smaller than the felt ukulele.

12. Cover the cardboard ukulele with a thin coat of glue and set it on the wrong side of the fabric page, underneath the felt ukulele. Pull the fabric as necessary while you glue cardboard.

13. Spread the small felt reinforcement pieces with a thin coat of glue and set them over the machine stitching on the elastic cords.

14. Place the ukulele under a heavy weight until thoroughly dry, about 6 to 8 hours.

15. Add tuning pegs and lettering with felt-tip markers. If you wish to trace the lettering, trace it on thin, see-through paper. Place the tracing upside down on a sheet of plain white paper. Go over the lettering with a transfer pencil, making a backward design. Turn over and transfer to the fabric.

Uu ukulele
pluck my strings

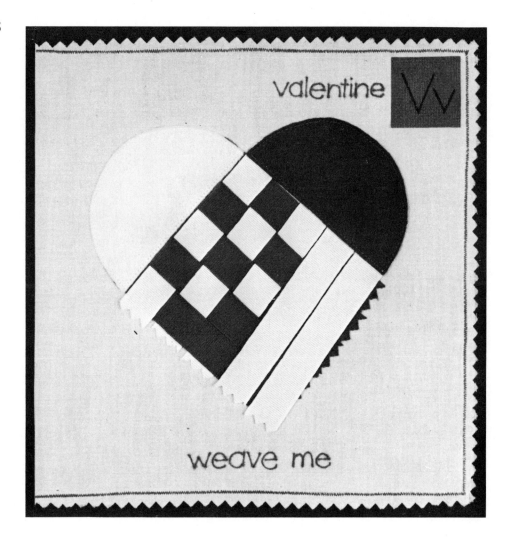

V for Valentine. It is best to make this valentine with grosgrain ribbon as it has enough body so it can be woven easily and it is sturdy enough to stand up under constant reweaving.

MATERIALS

Red felt
Thread to match
White felt
Thread to match
¾ yard of red grosgrain ribbon (⅝ of an inch)
¾ yard of white grosgrain ribbon (⅝ of an inch)

METHOD

1. Trace pattern for the semicircle on a sheet of paper.

2. Cut 1 white felt semicircle and 1 red felt semicircle.

3. Cut the red ribbon into 5 lengths about 5 inches each. Cut white ribbon into 5 lengths about 5 inches each.

4. Lay the lengths of white ribbon side by side on a flat surface, sides touching and edges approximately even. Spread glue along the straight edge of the red felt semicircle at least ½ of an inch up from the edge and set the felt on the pieces of ribbon so that the straight edge is perpendicular to them and covers ½ of an inch. (Do not worry if ribbon shows at the rounded edges of the felt.) Let dry.

5. Do the same things with the lengths of red ribbon on the white felt.

6. When glue is dry, trim ribbon as necessary so it won't show at the rounded edges of felt.

7. With a few dabs of glue, secure the 2 semicircles of the valentine in position on the fabric page, following the photograph. Sew the 2 felt pieces in place around the edges. Ribbon should hang loose.

8. Trim the ends of the ribbon with pinking shears. Ends of red ribbon should line up with outside piece of white ribbon and vice versa.

9. Add the lettering to the fabric page with a felt-tip marker. If you wish to trace the lettering, trace it on thin, see-through paper. Place the tracing upside down on a sheet of plain white paper. Go over the lettering with a transfer pencil, making a backward design. Turn over and transfer to the fabric.

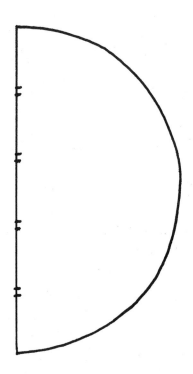

weave me

W for Wings. While this bird was designed as a crow and so was done in black felt with a yellow beak and gold-colored feet, he could be done in other colors. The wings lift up and down, as they are secured by a rubber band on the back and by paper fasteners to the body.

MATERIALS

Black felt (color optional)
Thread to match
Yellow felt (color optional)
Thread to match
Gold-colored felt (color optional)
Thread to match
1 plain white button or 1 eye button (available at most craft stores and some fabric stores)
2 brass paper fasteners
1 rubber band
Heavy cardboard

METHOD

1. Trace the separate patterns for the crow to a sheet of paper.

2. Pin the patterns for the 2 wings to black felt and cut around the edges.

3. Trace and cut 2 wings from heavy cardboard, using the same 2 patterns.

4. Lay the cardboard wings on a flat surface, with rounded sides almost touching and tips pointed outward.

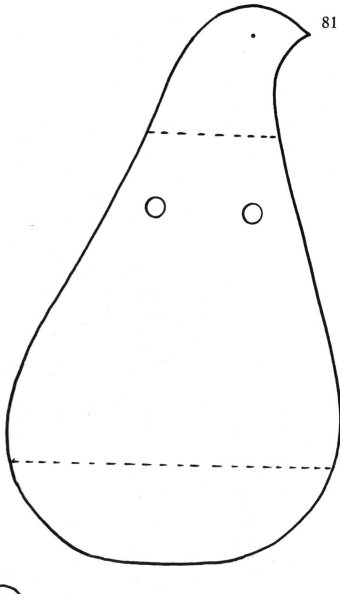

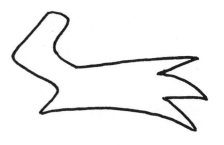

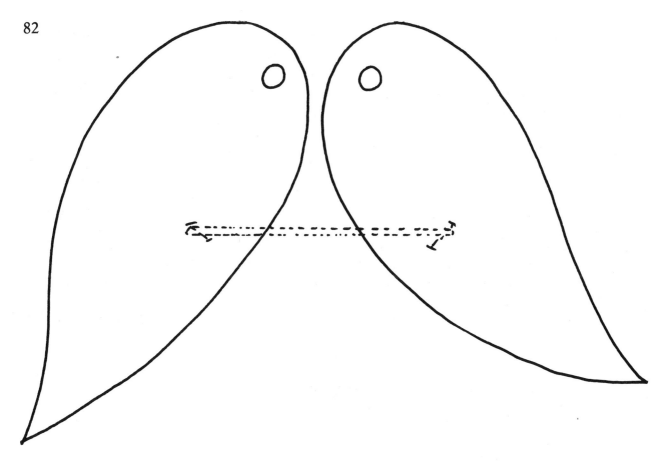

5. Place a circular rubber band in the middle of the two wings to connect them, as in the drawing. Staple or glue the rubber band in place temporarily.

6. Now spread the entire surface of the cardboard wings with glue and attach the felt wings to them. Set under a heavy weight until dry. This procedure will keep the rubber band securely in place.

7. Pin the pattern for the crow's body to black felt and cut around the edges along the lines of the pattern.

8. From heavy cardboard cut a reinforcement for the crow's body, eliminating the parts above and below the dotted lines on the pattern. Spread the cardboard reinforcement with glue and set it in position on the felt body. Place under a heavy weight until glue dries.

9. Pin the pattern for the crow's beak to yellow felt and cut around the edges along the lines of the pattern.

10. Pin the patterns for the 2 feet of the crow to gold-colored felt and cut around the edges along the lines of the pattern.

11. Remove the body and wings from beneath weights and with a paper punch make 1 hole in each of the rounded ends of the wings and 2 holes in the breast of the body, as shown in the pattern.

12. Attach the wings underneath the body

by putting brass paper fasteners through the holes.

13. Secure the crow in position to the fabric page with a few dabs of glue on the underneath side above and below the cardboard reinforcement, following the photograph for the placement. *Do not glue the cardboard to the page.*

14. Machine-stitch the parts of the crow to the fabric page above and below the cardboard.

15. With a few dabs of glue, set the crow's beak in position on the fabric page. Machine-stitch the beak to the fabric page.

16. With a few dabs of glue, secure the 2 feet in position on the fabric page. Machine-stitch the feet to the fabric page.

17. Add the lettering to the fabric page with a felt-tip marker. If you wish to trace the lettering, trace it on thin, see-through paper. Place the tracing upside down on a sheet of plain white paper. Go over the lettering with a transfer pencil, making a backward design. Turn over and transfer to the fabric.

X for Xmas. If you happen to have a small scrap of red and white striped cotton for the candy cane ornament, it is nice but it is not necessary. You can always use a red fabric-marker pen to make stripes on a piece of white cotton. The other ornaments are made of colored felt. And all of them can be unsnapped and stored in the box.

decorate me

MATERIALS

Red, green, black, yellow, and at least 1 other color of felt
Green thread
Red thread
Red and white striped cotton print (optional)
Heavy Pellon
5 snaps

METHOD

1. Trace the patterns for the tree and the 2 pieces for the box to a sheet of paper.

2. Trace the patterns for the ornaments to heavy Pellon by setting the Pellon on top of the patterns and going over the lines with a pencil. Separate the Pellon ornaments from each other by cutting between (not along) the lines.

3. Put the concave halves of the snaps aside and sew the convex halves inside the lines of the 5 Pellon ornaments, following the dotted lines on the patterns.

4. Spread the 5 Pellon ornaments with glue and place them on small pieces of colored felt, using yellow felt for the star and red and white striped cotton (set on the bias, if necessary) for

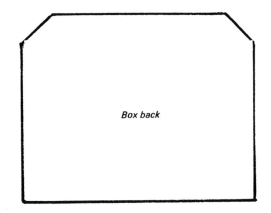

Box front

Box back

the candy cane. (NOTE: The glue and the Pellon will help to keep the cotton print from fraying, especially if you cut it after glue dries.)

5. Place the ornaments facedown on a flat surface. Take 5 spools of thread of the same height and put their holes over the prongs of the snaps. Place a heavy weight on top of the spools and proceed with next step.

6. Pin the pattern for the back of the box to black felt and cut around the edges.

7. Pin the pattern for the rectangle (front of box) to red felt and cut around the edges. Pin the red rectangle in place on the black felt box, following the photograph.

8. Pin the pattern for the tree to green felt and cut around the edges along the lines of the pattern. With a few dabs of glue, secure the tree in position on the fabric page, following the placement in the photograph. Machine-stitch the tree to the fabric page, going completely around the outside edges.

9. With a pencil, make dots where you would like to place the ornaments on the tree or follow the dotted lines for snaps on the pattern. Put a dot at the top for the star. Sew the 5 concave halves of the snaps to the places you have just marked.

10. With a few dabs of glue on the underneath side of the black felt, secure the box consisting of both red and black felt in position on the fabric page.

11. Machine-stitch the box to the fabric page, going completely around the outside edges. Do not sew along the top of the red rectangle. You now have another pocket in your fabric quiet book where you can hide occasional treats for the child such as raisins or nuts. This is also the box for storing the Christmas ornaments which go on the tree.

12. Remove the 5 ornaments from beneath the weight and cut them along the lines of the patterns.

13. Add the lettering to the fabric page with a felt-tip marker. If you wish to trace the lettering, trace it on thin, see-through paper. Place the tracing upside down on a sheet of plain white paper. Go over the lettering with a transfer pencil, making a backward design. Turn over and transfer to the fabric.

Y for Yarn. The yarn hair can be braided and tied with the attached ribbons. This is a really quiet activity which will keep a small child engrossed for long periods of time.

Black, brown, yellow, tan, or orange 2-ply yarn

Thread to match yarn

Cotton print fabric

Thread to match fabric

2 short lengths of colored ribbon

2 plain buttons or 2 eye buttons (available at most craft stores and some fabric stores)

Red thread for mouth (optional)

Black thread for face (optional)

1. Trace face and neck except eyes and hair and doll's collar on a sheet of white paper. Place the hand-traced pattern upside down on a sheet of plain white paper to help you see it better. Go over the design carefully on the back with a transfer pencil, making a backward design. Place the face in the middle of the fabric page, following the placement in the photograph. Transfer the pattern to fabric page by iron, as described in the general instructions.

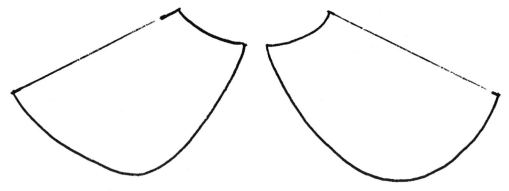

2. Go over the doll's face (except eyes and hair) with felt-tip markers, colored crayons, or a narrow and tight stitch on your zigzag machine. If you use crayons, press the design with a hot iron between 2 sheets of heavy brown paper before you proceed. If you use a zigzag stitch, place a sheet of paper under the fabric page as you work to keep the material from puckering.

3. Trace the collar patterns and pin them to a cotton print fabric and cut around the edges.

4. Secure the 2 collars in place on the fabric page with pins or hand basting. Do not use glue.

5. Place a sheet of paper under the fabric page as you work to keep the material from puckering. Machine-stitch around the edges of the collars with a narrow and loose zigzag stitch.

6. Set zigzag control to a wide and tight stitch. Machine-stitch again around the edges of the 2 collars. The second stitching should completely hide the first and extend beyond the edges of the print fabric to prevent fraying.

7. Cut about twenty 2½-inch lengths of yarn for the bangs. Lay the yarn pieces side by side on the forehead and pin in place. Machine-stitch the bangs to forehead at the top, just inside the curve of the doll's head.

(The stitches will be hidden by the procedures which follow.)

8. Cut about thirty 14-inch lengths of yarn. Smooth the yarn pieces next to each other, ends approximately even. Find the center of the yarn pieces and set it on the forehead, directly above the nose.

9. Smooth the yarn again so it looks like hair emerging from a center part and sew in place in the middle of the forehead.

10. Gently arrange the hair to fit the contour of her head and sew in place 4 more times, twice on each side. Sew across the yarn above the eyes and above the cheek.

11. Trim the bangs and side hair with scissors.

12. Sew bottons in position for eyes.

13. Braid the yarn hair in two plaits and tie them with small lengths of ribbon. Mark the place for the ribbon bow with a light pencil and tack the center of the ribbons there. When you give the book, leave one side unplaited.

14. Add the lettering to the fabric page with a felt-tip marker.

braid my hair

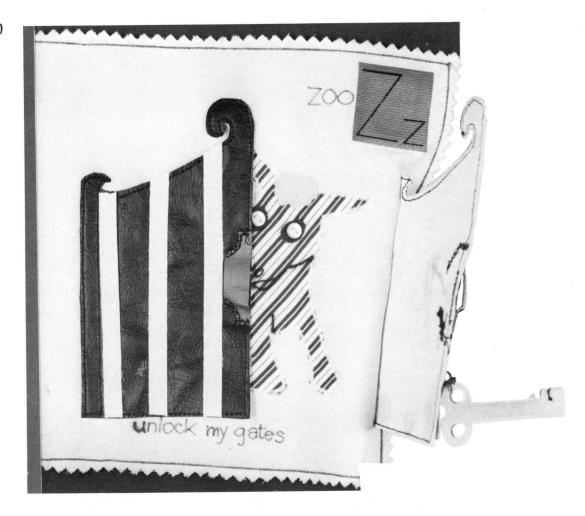

Z for Zoo. The gates of this zoo can be unlocked to reveal the appliquéd zebra within. These black vinyl or felt gates with white-grosgrain-ribbon stripes to represent real barred gates are a little fussy to make. You may wish to substitute some sort of striped fabric instead, but they do make a nice complement to the striped zebra.

Narrow, striped, cotton print fabric for zebra
Thread to match fabric
Contrasting felt for zebra's forelock
2 small pearl buttons for eyes
Red felt or vinyl for lock
¾ yard narrow white grosgrain ribbon
Heavy Pellon
Black felt or vinyl
Yellow felt (or other color) for key
Heavy cardboard
3-inch to 4-inch chain (available at most craft stores)

1. Trace the separate patterns for the zebra, lock, key, and felt eyes to a sheet of paper.

2. Pin the pattern for the zebra to the cotton print fabric so that the stripes run diagonally and cut around the edges along the lines of the pattern. With a pencil, draw the internal lines for the zebra.

3. Secure the zebra in place on the fabric page with pins or hand basting, following the photograph for placement. Do not use glue. Place a firm sheet of paper under the fabric page as you work to keep the material from puckering. Machine-stitch around the edges of the zebra with a narrow and loose zigzag stitch.

4. Set zigzag control to a wide and tight stitch. Machine-stitch again around the edges of the zebra. Second stitching should completely hide the first and extend beyond the edges of the print fabric to prevent fraying.

5. Cut a forelock for the zebra from colored felt and glue in place.

6. Go over the dotted lines of the zebra with felt-tip markers.

7. Sew 2 buttons in place for the zebra's eyes.

8. Set a piece of heavy Pellon on the pattern for the gates and trace the outside lines with a pencil. Cover the gates with a thin coat of glue. (Do not worry if the glue extends beyond the lines.) Set the uncut Pellon gates on a piece of black felt or vinyl and place under a heavy weight while you proceed with the next steps.

9. Trace the outside lines of the key (but not round holes) to a piece of heavy cardboard. And cut out the cardboard key. Spread the cardboard key with a thin coat of glue and

94 attach it to yellow felt. Set the uncut felt key under a heavy weight until the glue dries.

10. Pin the pattern for the lock to a piece of red felt or vinyl and cut around the outside edges. Then cut the lock in half along the dotted line.

11. If you are using felt rather than vinyl, you must reinforce the lock before you proceed. Machine-stitch each of the 2 halves of the felt lock to heavy Pellon around the outside edges. Trim the Pellon to match the edges of the felt.

12. Attach 1 end of the chain to 1 half of the lock. You can sew the chain to the lock with a needle and thread, or you can make a hole with a paper punch and attach the chain with a metal ring.

13. Remove the uncut Pellon and felt gates from beneath the weight. Cut the white grosgrain ribbon into 6 pieces, each from 5 inches to 4 inches long.

14. With a few dabs of glue, secure the ribbon to the felt sides of the gates in 6 vertical rows to resemble the spaces between bars of a gate. Machine-stitch the ribbon in place on the felt.

15. Turn the gates over so that the Pellon side is exposed. Machine-stitch completely around the edges of the 2 gates, just inside the pencil lines you have drawn on the Pellon. Cut out the gates along the lines you have drawn on the Pellon.

16. Set the gates on a flat surface so that they touch each other down the center.

17. Remove the uncut key from beneath the heavy weight. Cut the felt evenly along the edges of the cardboard. With a paper punch, make 3 holes in the felt key as shown in the pattern. Lay the key horizontally in the middle of the felt gates in the position shown in the second photograph.

18. Set the 2 halves of the lock on top of the key. Holding the 2 parts of the lock in position with one hand, work the key back and forth with the other to see how much fullness you must allow when you sew the lock to the gates. Remember that a small child will have greater difficulty pushing the key through the lock than you will and plan accordingly. Pin the 2 halves of the lock in position and remove the key.

19. Machine-stitch the 2 halves of the lock to the 2 halves of the gate along the top and bottom edges. Do not sew along the straight edges at the sides.

20. Attach the key to the other end of the metal chain as shown in the photograph.

21. Add the lettering to the fabric page with a felt-tip marker. If you wish to trace the lettering, trace it on thin, see-through paper. Place the tracing upside down on a sheet of plain white paper. Go over the lettering with a transfer pencil, making a backward design. Turn over and transfer to the fabric.

unlock my gates

Assembling the Book

Two of the designs in this book— the dinosaur and the igloo— if you make the latter with safety pins—require special techniques. This means that the pages sewn back to back with them—whether you are making an ABC book or not—must also be assembled in special ways. Please keep this fact in mind as you put the book together.

If you have eliminated the boxed ABC letters from the tops of the designs, you may assemble your pages in any order you wish. For an alphabet book to come out in proper order, however, you must sew your 14 completed fabric rectangles back to back as follows:

blank page—title page / back to back with A—Z

Y—B	"	C—X
W—D	"	E—V
U—F	"	G—T
S—H	"	I—R
Q—J	"	K—P
O—L	"	M—N

Set the fabric rectangles containing the dinosaur and the igloo (if you are using safety pins), plus the fabric rectangles you intend to sew back to back with them, aside for now.

Take 2 fabric rectangles and pin them back to back, smoothing out all wrinkles and keeping the corners even, lining up the pencil lines you drew at the very beginning, marking the rectangle 8 inches by 16 inches. If a side does not have clear pencil lines which you can follow on your machine, take the cardboard rectangle you made earlier as a pattern and trace around it on 1 of the fabric sides.

Using the pencil lines to guide you, sew around the 4 sides of the rectangle by machine. A decorative zigzag stitch with bright-colored thread works best. When the rectangles are sewn together, cut around them carefully with pinking shears ¼ of an inch outside the stitching.

Dinosaur Page. A small child will need an opening to the underside of this page for both hands. This means that you must allow hand space on the outside and bottom edges of the fabric page containing the dinosaur. Pin the wings/dinosaur page back to back with the earring/valentine page. Make certain that you have a clear pencil rectangle on both sides of the fabric and that they match perfectly.

On the dinosaur page, measure 1½ inches up from the lower right-hand corner and make a mark on the pencil border. Then measure 1½ inches from the corner on the bottom border and make a mark. Make a third mark 8 inches from the corner on the bottom border at the midway point.

Now turn the fabric over to expose the earring design. Measure 1½ inches up from the lower left-hand corner and make a mark on the pencil border. Next measure 1½ inches from the corner on the bottom border and make a mark. Make a third mark 8 inches from the corner on the bottom at the midway point between the earring and valentine designs.

Make certain that the marks you have made on the earring page correspond perfectly with those you have made on the dinosaur page.

Remove a few (but not all) of the pins joining the 2 fabric pages for the dinosaur and earring designs.

Using a zigzag stitch and bright-colored thread, sew along the pencil-drawn borders of the dinosaur and earring pages, 1 at a time, as follows:

Dinosaur Page. 1. From top right-hand corner along right-hand border to mark indicating 1½ inches from lower right-hand

corner. 2. From mark separating dinosaur and wings design along bottom border to mark indicating 1½ inches from lower right-hand corner.

Earring Page. 1. From top left-hand corner along left-hand border to mark indicating 1½ inches from lower left-hand corner. 2. From mark separating earring and valentine designs along bottom border to mark indicating 1½ inches from lower left-hand corner.

Now pin the pages back together very carefully so that the stitching matches exactly. Sew completely around the pages along the pencil marks for the borders, everywhere except where you have already stitched by machine. When you are through, all stitching should match evenly and you should have hand holes for the child along the outside and bottom edges.

Igloo Page. If you used safety pins, a small child will need access to the underside of the igloo page for one hand. Pin the igloo/rabbit page back to back with spider/hand pages, smoothing out all wrinkles and keeping the corners even. Make certain that you have a clear pencil rectangle on both sides of the fabric and that they match perfectly.

On the igloo page, measure 8 inches from the lower left-hand corner along the bottom border at the midway point between the igloo and rabbit designs and make a mark.

On the hand page, measure 8 inches from the lower right-hand corner along the bottom border at the midway point between the hand and spider designs and make a mark.

Remove a few (but not all) of the pins joining the 2 fabric pages for the hands and igloo designs. Using a zigzag stitch and bright-colored thread, sew along the pencil-drawn bottom borders of the igloo and hands designs separately, from the midway marks to the opposite corners.

Now pin the pages back together very carefully so that the stitching matches exactly. Sew completely around the pages along the pencil marks for the borders, everywhere except where you have already stitched by machine. When you are through, all stitching should match evenly and you should have a hand hole for the child along the bottom edge of the hands/igloo fabric page.

Covering the Book

1. With ruler and pencil, draw a rectangle measuring 9½ inches by 19 inches on the wrong side of a piece of vinyl plastic (or heavy fabric such as denim which has been reinforced with fusible Pellon). Sew along the pencil lines of the rectangle with a zigzag or decorative stitch (optional).

2. With pinking shears cut ½ of an inch outside the machine stitching on all 4 sides of the rectangle.

3. Set the rectangle wrong side up on a table. With ruler and pencil, draw a straight line through the width, marking the midway point of the inside of the cover.

4. Pin the fabric pages in place inside the cover. Before sewing them, check to see that they are assembled correctly and their midway points match the midway point of the cover and the corners of the fabric pages.

5. Machine-baste the fabric pages through all thicknesses to the cover at the center or spine of the book.

6. Sew down the center of the book, along the machine basting, with a narrow, tight zigzag stitch. Fold along stitching, cover on the outside.

7. If book seems especially bulky, reinforce it as necessary with additional stitching.